PENGUIN BOOKS

TALES FROM A CHILD OF THE ENEMY

Ursula Duba was born in Cologne, Germany, at the outbreak of World War II to a non-Jewish family. She grew up in postwar Germany and lived in Israel in the early sixties. In 1965 she came to the United States and lived in an Eastern European immigrant neighborhood in Brooklyn for several years. There she lived among Holocaust survivors and Jews who managed to escape but had lost family members in the Holocaust. Later on, she spent two years in the Southwest, and has been living in Stony Creek, Connecticut, since the mid-seventies. She is a writer and lecturer, working on a new collection of poems and on her first novel.

Tales from
a Child
of the Enemy

URSULA DUBA

Penguin Books

To my daughters Anneliese and Claudia
who gave me the gift of love
and to Tom for always believing in me

PENGUIN BOOKS
Published by the Penguin Group
Penguin Books USA Inc., 375 Hudson Street,
New York, New York 10014, U.S.A.
Penguin Books Ltd, 27 Wrights Lane, London W8 5TZ, England
Penguin Books Australia Ltd, Ringwood, Victoria, Australia
Penguin Books Canada Ltd, 10 Alcorn Avenue,
Toronto, Ontario, Canada M4V 3B2
Penguin Books (N.Z.) Ltd, 182–190 Wairau Road,
Auckland 10, New Zealand

Penguin Books Ltd, Registered Offices:
Harmondsworth, Middlesex, England

First published in the United States of America
by Twin Soul Productions 1995
Published in Penguin Books 1997

1 3 5 7 9 10 8 6 4 2

AUTHOR'S NOTE
Names, places, and incidents have been altered to protect the privacy of
actual persons.

LIBRARY OF CONGRESS CATALOGING IN PUBLICATION DATA
Duba, Ursula.
Tales from a child of the enemy/Ursula Duba.
p.   cm.
ISBN 0 14 058.787 X (pbk.)
1. Holocaust survivors — Poetry.   2. Holocaust, Jewish (1939–1945) —
Poetry.   3. War victims — Poetry.   4. World War, 1939–1945 — Poetry.
I. Title.
PS3554.U239T35   1997
811'.54 — dc21   96–36893

Printed in the United States of America
Set in Cochin
Designed by Jennifer Ann Daddio

Contents

The Child of the Enemy

my Greek friend comforted me
when she heard
that my father died
she knows how it feels
to be five thousand miles away
and not have anybody to cry with

she rushes to my house
with homemade bread
a chicken dish
flavored with rosemary and thyme
she puts her arms around me
and I cry into her shoulder

my Greek friend remembers
the occupation of her land
by my people
she remembers wounds and scars
of her people tortured by Nazis
men taken away
never to return
mass executions
in her native village
in the mountains of Greece

when Iraq is bombed
and I tell her
how enraged I am
at attacks at civilians

no matter what the reasons
because I remember how it feels
to be a child of six
and live in a city
hit by carpet bombing
surrounded by adults
half crazed with terror and hunger
and when I tell her
how it feels
to crawl out from under
after an air raid
to look down the street
and see whose house was hit
and how I cannot forget
adults whispering in horror
that phosphor bombs
missed the railroad station
and hit the slums instead
and people running through the streets
like living torches
screaming
until they jumped
into the river
to drown themselves

my voice chokes
and tears run down my face
my Greek friend does not comfort me
when she sees my tears of rage
at more suffering of civilians—
my Greek friend leans back
and I see in her eyes

that I am the child of her enemies
she remembers the atrocities
committed by my people
in her native village
in the mountains of Greece

Carpet Bombing

she knew what a bomb was
at age five
after all
sirens had warned her
of bombing attacks
at night
for as long as she could remember
she had gotten used to
being dragged out of bed
slept in her clothes
until finally
she her six siblings and parents
stayed in the tiny
underground bomb shelter

today
the adults
were more agitated than usual
as she caught the word
carpet bombing
again and again
and couldn't understand
why this word
was causing such terror
while she tried to figure out
what kinds of carpets
were going to fall
from the sky —
long narrow carpets
also called runners

like the one in the hallway
staircase carpets
firmly held in place
by shiny brass rods
small carpets
like the one
in front of her bed
or large carpets with intricate designs
and rich colors
like the one in the living room
which was treated with such reverence

but she never saw any carpets
after the bombing
when they cautiously opened the front door
to see whose house had been hit
once the all-clear siren had gone off
and nobody told
the five-year-old
where the carpets had been dropped
during the carpet bombing

The Easter Bunny

on Easter 1945
their mother explained to them
after they had lived
in the bomb shelter
for six months
that the Easter Bunny
couldn't come this time
the carpet bombing prevented him
from visiting the homes
where children lived
and hiding colored eggs
and sweets
for them to find

he'll make it up to you
in peacetime
she added

the children
who only knew wartime
who had never known
the easy availability of anything
who thought the adults were crazy
when they reminisced
about peacetime
this unimaginable time
when you could go to a store
and buy whatever you wanted
the children
understood

that the Easter Bunny
couldn't hide colored eggs
and sweets
during carpet bombing

still
all day
they looked furtively
behind and underneath things
explored possible Easter Bunny hiding places
being careful
not to let on to anybody
what they were looking for
or that they were looking for anything —
but deep down they believed
that the Easter Bunny
had defied war and carpet bombing
and had hid colored eggs
and sweets for them
somewhere

A Slice of Bread

in early 1945
in Germany
her father divided
the daily loaf of bread
into eighteen thin slices
for nine of them
seven children
age three to ten
and two adults

in the morning
there was a scraping of margarine
on the slice of bread
in the evening
a scraping of jam

there was no other food
all day

hunger became a relentless companion
and one day
at noon
the six-year-old
the middle child
small for her age
seeing the evening ration
in a corner of the bomb shelter
told her mother
how hungry she was

and asked her
for another slice of bread

there
eat it quickly
her mother said
before anybody sees you

in the evening
her father discovered
that a slice of bread
one person's dinner
was missing
and interrogated everybody

yes she said
Mommy gave me the bread
because I told her
how hungry I was

a wave of fury
came over the father
who hadn't had a full meal in a long time
how dare you
ask your mother
for another slice of bread
he screamed
don't you know
that someone else will go hungry
because of your greed
your lack of consideration for others
your selfishness

and he grabbed the six-year-old
all skin and bones
and hit her
again and again

he hit her
for his own intolerable hunger
he hit her
for the SS who came to see him
every day
trying to force him into the army
he hit her
for the fear he suffered
of being discovered
operating a radio receiver
with which he listened
to enemy forces
and was illegally aware
of the true status of the war
an act of high treason
for which he could be shot
instantly
he hit her
because he was angry with the Allied Forces
for taking so long to come and liberate them
he hit her
for the rage he felt
because his neighbors had threatened him
with denunciation
when he hadn't believed in the final victory
while they were drunk with pride
after conquering half of Europe
in the *Blitzkrieg*

he hit her
because his wife
didn't have enough sense
and had given in
to the demand of a small child
he hit her
for all the indignity and injustices
he had suffered from his Nazi colleagues and superiors
because he wasn't a member of the party
he hit her
because he was terrified
of the nonstop bombing
he hit her
because he couldn't feed his family
and was scared
they would starve to death
and he hit her
because he was a coward
who had never openly expressed his anger
and vehement rejection of the Hitler regime
to his colleagues and superiors

she didn't understand
what she had done wrong
and why she had received this beating
but never again
for the rest of her childhood
did she ever
ask her mother
or her father
for anything

A Child's Dream

she was six and a half
at the end of WWII
and didn't have the words
to talk about
the horrors she had experienced

her mother and father
aunts and uncles
and all adults she knew
age thirty-five and up
had lived through
two world wars
and her grandfather
age seventy-eight
had lived through three wars

they talked about the atrocities of war
endlessly

soon
she learned at school
that in her part of the world
people had slaughtered
each other
with steadfast ferocity
and ever-increasing efficiency
for over a thousand years

by age ten
she had learned enough

in history and geography
to know
that there were countries
far away
which didn't have wars
regularly
and she made up her mind
that she'd find such a place
and go there
and be safe
from war
forever

Being Groomed for Higher Education

when she was seven years old
her mother told the teacher
that she wanted her daughter
to receive a higher education
and would the teacher
please see to it
that her daughter
studied hard
so that she would pass
the demanding entrance exam
to the *Gymnasium*

the old teacher
who herself had only finished 8th grade
plus two years of a teachers' seminary
didn't think that anybody
should go further than she had
especially a girl —
what had been good enough for her
sixty years ago
was certainly good enough
for anybody else

the old teacher disliked
the seven-year-old girl
who had a mind of her own
had too much imagination
talked during class
and made the other kids laugh
with jokes and wisecracks —

so she picked her out
for special treatment

every day
she found fault with her
and called her
in front of the class —
an error in arithmetic
a spelling mistake
dirty fingernails
a stain on her dress
or catching her whisper
to another girl
and the tall old teacher
with the straight back
the immaculate hairdo
and the starched shirt front
would hit her
on the back
with the flat of her hand
again and again
while saying
so you think
you'll pass that exam
look at yourself
you are stupid
and dirty
you'll never pass the tests

the little girl
tried hard
not to make mistakes
in arithmetic

and spelling
to have clean fingernails
no stains on her dress
and especially
not to whisper wisecracks
to the other kids

but try as she might
the teacher
continued to find fault —
she was one of seven children
and there was nobody
to make sure
she washed her face
and cleaned her fingernails
before going to school
the bath water
was only heated once a week
and the school dress
had to last all week
and sitting still for hours
made her restless

at the beginning
of the daily beatings
she had complained
to her mother
but quickly learned
how unwise that was —
you must have done something wrong
otherwise the teacher wouldn't hit you
her mother had said
and she had received

an additional beating
at home

one day
the old teacher
told the class
about the Celts
and homework that day
was a composition
about those ancient people

the little girl
who was an avid reader
had seen a book
about the Celts in the library
and added many details
about the life
of that old culture
to her composition
which the teacher hadn't mentioned

she was so eager
to show the teacher
what additional information
she had found
but the old teacher
wasn't pleased at all
how dare you write
what I haven't lectured
she said
and that day
the beating
was particularly bad

sometimes
when she was conscientiously
doing her homework
she would dream
that the old teacher
would peer through the window
and would see her
diligently bent over her desk
writing neat rows of figures
using her best penmanship
for the composition required
and she hoped
that the teacher would realize
that she wasn't bad
and she would praise her instead
and the beatings
and the daily humiliation
in front of the class
would stop

finally
the day of the entrance exam arrived
and much to the little girl's surprise
she passed

the little girl
was very pleased
and couldn't wait
to run to the old teacher
and tell her with joy
and excitement
guess what Miss Wadenberg
I passed

but Miss Wadenberg
wasn't pleased at all
and said
in a few months
your new teachers
will find out
how stupid you really are
and then
they'll send you back to me

nobody will send me back to you
the little girl said to herself
and then added
when I am grown up
and am enjoying the life I want
you'll be long dead
and eaten up by worms

My First Orange

the first oranges
which appeared in German stores
two or three years after WWII
were sold by the piece
and cost the equivalent of
ten loaves of sourdough bread
two pounds of meat
or thirty pounds of potatoes

since we were a family of nine
it didn't make much sense
my mother explained to me
to buy a single orange
at such an exorbitant price
and then divvy it up
into nine portions

but a neighbor of ours
who only had one child
went out and purchased
that exotic fruit

the neighbor
whose husband was an unskilled laborer
told my mother
that she didn't care
how much this orange cost
she wanted her son
her only child
who had been deprived for so long

who had never experienced
the abundance of the prewar years
to taste an orange
but given its price
the eating of this orange
had to be done with the proper decorum
and in the right setting

so she brought her son
over to our house
and while we stood around in a circle
she showed her son
how to cut the skin lengthwise
into equally measured sections
then peel them off
and finally break off a section of the fruit
and eat it
in front of us
while we
all seven of us children
and my mother
watched him
our mouths watering

yes we could see the orange
yes we could smell its fine fragrance
no we couldn't taste it

that was my first orange

Ruins

five years after the end of WWII
the family went on a trip
in two canoes
on the river Mosel
a lovely region in Germany
inhabited by Celts in ancient times
later conquered and colonized
by the Romans
who had introduced
the cultivation of grapes
and the knowledge of fine wines
more than two thousand years ago

after the defeat of the Roman Empire
feudal lords
built fortresses and castles
on top of the hills along the river
with the help of forced labor
by the peasants

in nineteen fifty
most of these fortresses and castles
where many battles have been fought
for hundreds of years
are in a state of shabby disrepair
and look like ruins to the children

the parents
who experienced crushing defeat

of their nation
in WWI and again in WWII
are eager to teach their children
about the long and glorious past
of their country
still mostly in rubble
and point out
famous ruin after ruin
as they glide on the water

they tell the children
who had built the castle
(the peasants who had done
the actual work
remained nameless)
how long the house of so-and-so
had reigned in it
what battles had been fought
and when it had fallen
the children
who are growing up
in a city
flattened by three years of bombing
don't understand
the obsession
with which the parents talk
about those ruins

what's with them
they ask each other
after all
we live among ruins

we play in ruins
the adults constantly complain about the ruins
and wasn't the purpose of this trip
to get away from the ruins
and to enjoy the countryside

The Good Old Days

in 1958
at her first job
age twenty
most of her colleagues
were fifteen years older than she
had been seduced
by exuberant outdoor adventures
exciting camping trips
swimming running and folk dancing
superbly organized by the Hitler Youth
and had heard Hitler speak
many times
of the glorious nation
he was going to create
in their country
with a new society
the Thousand Year Reich
by getting rid of
all those
he considered racially impure
and inferior

long after the rubble of WWII
had been cleared away
after the citizens had rebuilt their cities
with the same dedication
skill and expertise
used to build elaborate railroad systems going east
and efficient facilities
for the extermination of millions

fifteen years earlier
those older colleagues
regularly reminisced
about the good old days
the streets used to be safe
they said
even late at night
there was much less crime
no faggots corrupting our youth
the *Autobahn* absolutely perfect
everybody knew their place
and students weren't allowed
to demonstrate

nobody mentioned
the *Kristallnacht*
people having to wear yellow stars
arrests in the middle of the night
deportations
the constant fear
of being denounced by a neighbor
the reign of terror
the Holocaust

one day
they saw her having lunch
at a restaurant
with some people
whose language they didn't recognize

they are Israelis
you say
don't you know

they exclaim
in horror
about dirtying German blood

the good old days

The Victims

she was seven
in 1945
at the end of WWII
in Cologne Germany
one of the seven thousand
from the prewar count of seven hundred thousand

quite a few had died
but most had fled
the relentless carpet bombing
of the Allied Forces

the two-thousand-year-old city
founded by the Romans
was in rubble
people came crawling out of holes
hungry
wondering what to do next
food was scarce
housing nonexistent
the black market flourishing

what she remembers most
fifty years later
is the constant lament
she heard
year in and year out
even long after
the rubble had been cleared
Cologne and the rest of Germany

rebuilt
splendidly so
with generous help of the Marshall Plan
everything was gleaming
with newness
and looked perfect
a decade after WWII

it was called
the economic miracle
and the very word
filled the German hearts
with pride

still
while acquisitions of new
living room and bedroom sets
were endlessly discussed
there was always an opportunity
to remember and bemoan
the horrible hardships
suffered during the war —
whose house had been bombed
how their cats and dogs had disappeared
people carting heirlooms off to the countryside
to exchange for
   a bag of potatoes
   a pound of lard
   a few cans of sardines

resentment is still alive
against the farmers

who had become rich
because of city folks' misery

one neighbor
couldn't forget
how her weekly ration
of half an ounce of butter
had melted right into
the heavy brown paper
the store owner
had used
when weighing the dab of butter
on a hot day in July —
when she got home
there was nothing left
but a large greasy stain

she still sees the rage
in the neighbor's face
the humiliation
the indignity of it all
there was no winning
between the government regulations
setting up inhuman rations
and the store owners
who controlled distribution
and got fat
in the process

one neighbor's wife
had fled to a village in the country
with her three children

but the water had been contaminated
and she died of typhoid
leaving the small children behind
for the father to find
when he returned years later
from captivity in Russia

then there were stories
about the American soldiers
who had defecated
into the sauerkraut crocks
which were followed
by whispered stories about the women
who were raped
and detailed accounts about
the atrocities committed
by the Russians

they saw themselves as victims
all of them
for as long as they lived
never once did they consider
the hardships
the devastations
the atrocities
the unspeakable horror
their country
their soldiers
their *Führer*
the Nazis
the SS
had inflicted on tens of millions of people

in other countries
in their pursuit
to conquer the world

and when the increasing prosperity
allowed vacations
in surrounding countries
they were surprised
always surprised
when store owners
and restaurant personnel
in Holland or France
didn't want to serve them
when they heard them
speaking German

they couldn't understand
wouldn't understand
that anybody
could be cross with them —
the hardworking Germans
who had suffered so much

fifty years later
when she hears yet another story
about their horrible suffering
during a rare visit
to Germany
she asks them
why they were so surprised
about the carpet bombing
the hatred
the acts of revenge

and the hostility
by those
whose countries they had invaded
bombed
plundered
and whose people
they had tortured and killed

a traitor
they called her
for posing such a question
and heartless
for not showing
enough empathy
for their suffering

Aunt Selma

she was tall
and on Sundays
dressed
in her only suit
extravagant hat
excited to leave the house
to go to church
her only outing
a stunning looking woman
in her mid-thirties

in 1945
Aunt Selma and her sister Edith
were grudgingly offered
two tiny attic rooms
in our house
after their apartment
had turned into rubble
during one of the last
carpet bombings
in Cologne

everything
about the sisters
was mysterious
Aunt Edith
had a son
and an absent husband
who had been taken prisoner of war
by the Russians

but when his name was mentioned
the adults
always exchanged glances
and her son Otto
nine years old at the time
was treated with great suspicion
as if he had
committed some unforgivable crime
and had a blemish
that nothing
absolutely nothing
could remove

Aunt Selma
in her threadbare
everyday clothes
never left the house
and stayed mostly in her little attic room
darning socks and mending clothes
in the most meticulous way
almost like embroidery
which earned her much derision
from the other adults

there was no affection
shown by my father
to either of his sisters

one day
sitting at the table
Aunt Selma made a strange sound
and slipped under the table
the adults all jumped up

and within seconds
she was carried
into an adjoining room
the door to that room
was firmly shut

I was seven at the time
and very scared
at seeing Aunt Selma
eyes wide open
tongue sticking out
rigid

questions to answers
were responded to with orders
that I should not mention
what I had seen
ever
I was made to understand
that if anybody
found out
about Aunt Selma's affliction
it would shed
a terrible light
on all of us

being of sound genetic stock
was all-important
in the time of the master race

Aunt Selma's epileptic seizures continued
eventually

I lost my fear
she always seemed fine when she came to

why isn't Aunt Selma married
I once asked my mother
and why doesn't she ever go anywhere
how can she marry
with this terrible affliction
my mother answered
and what if she had a fit
outside the house
then all would know
about the family shame
no no
she has to stay at home
it's bad enough
that we are all
in continuous dread
that Aunt Selma
will have a seizure
on Sunday
in church

things grew tense in our house
over the next few months
soon there were allegations
that Aunt Selma had been seen
taking potatoes
out of our potato bin
in the root cellar

speculations were uttered aloud
whether sly Aunt Edith

had put her sister
up to this potato theft
or whether Aunt Selma
actually had the intelligence
despite her affliction
and the malice
brought on by the affliction
to plan this crime herself

in due course
we children were forbidden
to play with Cousin Otto
even though
he didn't have a contagious disease
had not been caught
stealing potatoes
and appeared to me
to be a regular boy of nine

you'll understand why
when you are grown up
my mother told me

years later
I found out
that Aunt Edith
who had been responsible
for taking care
of her hypochondriac mother
and her afflicted sister
for years
which kept her out of school
prevented her from leading a normal life

and learning a profession
while her older siblings
gathered prestigious degrees from well-known universities
was finally allowed to leave the house
at age nineteen
after her mother's death
and went to visit an aunt and uncle in Bavaria

the uncle promptly seduced her
and Cousin Otto
was the unfortunate fruit
of that seduction

nobody ever expressed
outrage
toward the uncle
who had committed
incest with his young niece

soon whispering behind closed doors
became the norm
and things grew worse and worse
in our house
within the year
Aunt Edith Aunt Selma and Cousin Otto
were asked to leave

they found a room
in a partially destroyed building
in the center of town

six months later
I was told

that Aunt Selma had died
and the funeral was to be
the day after next

I pleaded with my mother
to tell everybody
to wait longer
didn't they know
that Aunt Selma always came to

nobody listened
and for years I was convinced
that Aunt Selma
whose affliction had to be hidden
from the world
who never had a normal life
who couldn't get the medication she needed
in the chaos of the postwar years
had been buried alive

Blind Date

it was the year of the World's Fair
in Brussels 1958
she had finally received permission
from her strict father
who maintained
that only married women
should travel abroad
accompanied by their husbands
to visit her aunt in Antwerp
a hundred miles from her native town
at age nineteen and a half

the aunt
much younger than her mother
and open to notions of romance and adventure
had talked to the daughter
of a neighbor
whose boyfriend had a younger brother
who was promptly enlisted
to be her blind date
for the evening

she had spent all afternoon
getting ready for this blind date
her first
had tried a dozen different hairstyles
had applied pancake makeup
eye shadow
black eyeliner
rouge

lipstick
all things she wasn't normally
allowed to use
finally she had put on
her new narrow pale yellow dress
and wrapped a black stole with fringes
around her shoulders

she felt very grown up in this getup
very worldly
very sophisticated
with the makeup
the pale yellow dress
the black stole with fringes
her long dark hair
swept to one side of her face
drinking whiskey
in a nightclub in Brussels
with the neighbor's girl and her boyfriend
and her blind date
who was a year older than she
and very handsome

her aunt had told her
that the two brothers were Jewish

she'd never met a Jew in Germany
hardly knew what it meant
and vaguely thought
it was a religion
like being Catholic or Protestant
just more rare
like being Hindu

her handsome date
and she were dancing
cheek to cheek
to a slow blues melody
when he asked her
what do you think of Auschwitz

she thought he meant Austerlitz
and replied
that she wasn't much of a history buff
and didn't care about Napoleon and his battles

back at their table
he told her about Auschwitz
Hitler
the Nazis
gas chambers
and six million of his people killed

he himself had been hidden
in a monastery

the handsome young man
couldn't believe
that this educated young woman
really didn't know
about the atrocities committed
by her country

there was no more dancing
cheek to cheek
that night

instead they talked
till daybreak

she was shocked
bewildered
felt confusion
horror
shame
anger
rage

till the end of her life
she would have to prove
that she wasn't one of them
   like the ones who had kept silent
   like the ones who had colluded
   like the ones who had participated

she felt outraged
that she hadn't been told
about this
by her parents
her teachers
the parish priest

thirteen years of school
and nobody had told her about this

three years of history alone
had been spent on learning
about the Greeks and Romans
battles had to be memorized

endlessly
invasions
plundering
sacking of towns
conquering
it was called
the victors
were always called
glorious and superior
and the conquered
weak and inferior
deserved to be sold into slavery

the German soldier is the best in the world
her old Nazi history teacher
used to say at the end
of each class
twice a week

he made them sound so noble
courageous and virtuous
those German soldiers
he praised twice a week
for three years

the old history teacher
didn't mention
the German soldiers
who forced
tens of thousands of men and women
to dig their own graves
and then shot them

after nine years of studying
Antiquity
the Dark Ages
the Middle Ages
the Renaissance
the Age of Enlightenment
the Industrial Revolution
the Nineteenth Century
ten minutes before graduation
the teacher had told the class
that WWI started in 1914 and ended in 1918
that Hitler was elected in 1933
that WWII had started in '39 and ended in '45
and that was all they learned
about the history of the twentieth century
whereupon the teacher had dismissed them
with good wishes for the future

after she returned to Cologne
from the trip abroad
she scoured the libraries
for information on what happened
between 1933 and 1945
she found books
describing unspeakable horrors
committed by her people
and saw photographs
showing laughing men
torturing Jews Gypsies homosexuals non-Aryans

the Germans
her people
who like to call themselves

the people of poets and thinkers
had kept meticulous records
of the atrocities committed
against people
they considered
degenerate and inferior
and who consequently
deserved to be dehumanized
tortured
and murdered

she brought the books home
threw them at her parents
yelling at them
how could you let this happen
what did you do to stop this
how can you send me
off into the world
without telling me about these horrors

her parents
of course
told her
like millions of other German parents
that they hadn't known about any of this
and that they didn't do it
and besides
did she know
how the French
had treated the Algerians
and the English
the people in India

we Germans
are not the only ones
who have done wrong
they yelled back

they expressed no sorrow
at the suffering inflicted on others
and couldn't understand
the shame she felt
the horror
of having grown up
among murderers

Family Secrets

a bird
the old woman says
on the telephone
to her daughter
three thousand miles
across the ocean
a bird
she says
does not dirty its own nest

the old woman is dying
hooked up to machines
voice so weak
it's hardly recognizable
the old woman
still lashes out
at her daughter
by telephone

the daughter
herself the mother
of grown-up daughters
who called
to wish her mother well
called
to say I care
the daughter
is taken aback
feels slapped

in the face
again

the daughter hears
in the command of her mother
that the murderer among us
has to be protected
at all costs
after all
he is one of us

the daughter
left home
thirty hears ago
escaped a childhood
of abuse
and rejection
and fled
the place of her birth
when she discovered
that she had grown up
in a country
of mass murderers

now she tries to distract
her mother
with the pleasant news
that Cousin Trudi's daughter Irene
is visiting
and is a lovely young woman
don't tell her
about the past
the old woman commands

mother
the daughter replies
please
we are in the kitchen
baking cookies
I have heard
the old woman counters
that you do talk
about the past
and
she continues
your father and I
we didn't know
what they did to the Jews
in the concentration camps
sure
we knew about them
but not
what went on inside

we didn't do anything wrong
besides
what do you know
about
how dangerous it was
to open one's mouth
you think
it was so easy
to speak out
and how terrified we were
in the bomb shelters
night after night
the sirens

cutting through you like a knife
you never knew
whose house would be hit
and who would have taken us in
with seven children
and what do you know
about hunger
they were not the only ones
who suffered
we suffered too

the old woman
hooked up to machines
near death
is afraid
that when she closes
her eyes
the daughter
will talk
the truth
will come out
that this was not
a loving
nice
respectable
family
that five
of the seven children
were not wanted
were told so
every day
were put down
with cruel derision

were beaten
mercilessly
for almost twenty years
by her husband
their father
while she
silently watched
never once saying
stop it

no
the old woman
cannot trust
that daughter
to keep quiet
the daughter
who left the country
and lived
in the land
of the murdered —
how can she live in Israel
among un-Christian people
the mother had said

that daughter
has always been
disobedient
and has never cared
about the country's
and the family's honor
the old woman
with the facade
of stony silence

about the past
who has lived
in agonizing denial
for eighty years
with all her children participating
except that one
the one
who ran away
the old woman
hooked up to machines
weighed down by guilt
the old woman
is terrified

The Sundial

even though the seven-year-old girl
was born in Germany
she was called
the foreigner
because her parents were refugees
from Eastern Europe
of distant German parentage

at school
she was relegated to the back row
was hardly ever asked
to answer questions
never had a chance
to recite a poem
sing a song
to participate

one morning
the teacher
taught the children in class
about the sundial
and since it was a bright
and sunny day
she asked the children
to step outside
for a demonstration

the foreign girl
was asked to step into a circle
her shadow was duly marked with a rock

then the children
and the teacher
went back to their classroom
but when the foreign girl
wanted to join them
she was told by the teacher
no you stay here
you are the sundial of the day

every hour the class stepped outside
and marked the changing
sundial's shadow with a rock
then all went back
into the classroom

the seven-year-old foreign girl
stood in the center of the circle
all morning
she felt so honored
at being chosen
so glad to participate

when she got hot
and restless
and started to wonder
whether it truly was an honor
to be left outside
alone
she remembered
what her mother used to say
listen to what the teacher says
don't make any waves
always be obedient

it had taken her parents
five years of wandering
from country to country
and long stays in labor camps
before they finally arrived
in the country of their ancestral origin

at noon the teacher
pointed to the sundial
so that all could see
there was no shadow
and while the other children
enjoyed their recess
the foreign girl
continued standing in the sun
alone
her day of finally being noticed
by the teacher
her day of glory
had turned into a day of pain and confusion

The Baker's Story

when the bakery opened downstairs
five flights below our apartment
we smelled the aroma
through the open windows

the baker was a jovial man
in his early sixties
reddish-white hair
blue eyes
high color in his cheeks
who made it his business
to get to know his customers by name
and who never tired to tempt me
with his challah
dense Russian bread
mountains of cookies
juicy apple turnovers —
the baker always had a smile
a compliment and a cookie
for my little girls
and best regards to Mr. Pollak

the baker's wife would say
maybe Mrs. Pollak wants to save the cookies for
                                        after dinner
but the baker would wave away such silly concerns —
he wanted to see the children's eyes light up
and their little hands
reach out for the treat

the baker's wife was a skinny little woman
her hair hidden under a handkerchief
dressed in plain gray clothes
she scurried around
to please her husband
reminded him to go upstairs
and eat his lunch
wrapped up bread and cakes
for the customers

the baker and his wife had been born in Poland
and they had numbers on their arms

when we moved to Long Island
and my husband went to see the baker
to say good-bye
he didn't come back for quite a while

the baker
whose name I don't remember
but whose numbered arm
I still see in front of me
told my husband
that he reminded him
of one of his children
who died in the camps
like all his children
like all his family
like all his wife's children
and her whole family
this was their second marriage
he told my husband
they had met at Auschwitz

because of my husband's resemblance
to one of his children
the baker asked and probed
into my husband's roots
father born in Romania
great-grandfather born in Poland —
the baker's eyes lit up
could it be
that he had found a distant relative
just one
so many still unaccounted for
but my husband didn't know names
of great-uncles and cousins in Poland
he never met any of his family
he himself had been born in Persia
the child of refugees —
his father had fled to Persia
from the Nazis in Romania
the Russians made him a prisoner of war there
put him in a death camp in Siberia
and when he came back
after seven years of captivity
he had become a man of silence
and hid behind newspapers —
there was no idle chatter
about brothers and sisters
cousins aunts and uncles

months later
when I go to Brooklyn
to pick up a special order of Russian bread
the baker who greets me
in a broken voice

is an old man
bent over
thin
red-rimmed eyes

my wife died
he says
I am so sorry
I didn't know she was ill
I say
the baker motions me to the back of the store
and whispers
she wasn't
nothing really wrong with her
just a little pain
the doctor sent her to the hospital for X rays
THEY killed her there
he says
and with a furtive look he says
so low that I can barely hear him
the Nazis have infiltrated the hospitals in *Amerika*

may he rest in peace

Still Looking

I was a greenhorn in nineteen sixty-five
had only lived in the USA
for barely six months
when a neighbor told me
I could make some extra money
selling Avon cosmetics
in my neighborhood

I had never in my life
sold anything
but it sounded so easy
and tempting
that I agreed
after all I was in *Amerika*
the land of unlimited possibilities

most of my neighbors were refugees
from Eastern Europe
displaced persons camps
Holocaust survivors
full of hope
for a new beginning and a safe place
for their children

Mrs. Weihs was one of my customers
a no-nonsense woman
who ordered shampoo
soaps and deodorants
one day I met her daughter
a lovely girl of twelve or thirteen

say hello to Mrs. Pollak
her mother told her
but the daughter just stared
and disappeared into her room
she was very young
for a couple in their fifties
Mrs. Weihs turned to me with a sigh
I don't know what to do with her
first she wants her own room
and we move into this apartment
now she wants her own telephone

imagine her own telephone
I've never even had a room of my own
my two sisters and I
used to share a large bed until I married
and how will I know
what she says on the telephone
it's not that I don't want her to be happy
that's the reason we came here
but I am her mother
I have to know

Mrs. Kaufman isn't given to
lavish purchases either
but she is a steady customer
always offers a cup of coffee
and a piece of cake
she was born in Vienna
so we speak German

I was an only child
she says

and suddenly
I see a prematurely aged woman
transform herself
into a little girl
with a gleam in her eyes
when she tells me
how her mother
who was quite plump
used to chase after her with a hairbrush
when she had been bad —
along the corridor
in and out of the bedroom
through the living room
finally into the dining room
around and around the table

her father would say
why can't you two get along
and be civilized
my father didn't understand
she says
with a twinkle in her eyes
that this is how we loved each other
me teasing her
she chasing after me

one afternoon she tells me
how she left Vienna in 1939
on the last children's boat
allowed to enter Palestine
she was thirteen years old
and never saw anybody of her family again

Mrs. Berkovitz is my very best customer
her face is crisscrossed with fine wrinkles
and the dyed hair looks harsh
next to her skin
do you think it will work
she asks
leafing through sales catalogues
fascinated by promises
that bags under eyes will disappear over night
along with crows' feet
and the overall sagging of the skin
so I write up good orders

Mr. Berkovitz hovers in the background
while we study claims
of expensive skin products
he barely mumbles hello
but I feel
he is watching me
and I wonder whether he is angry with me
for selling his wife expensive potions
with promises for a long-lost youth

one day
Mr. Berkovitz greets me in an almost jovial manner
asks permission to inquire about my family
I am mystified but oblige him
toss out names
it's my father's family
he wants to know about
did he have sisters
what were their names

Henrietta I say was the oldest
then there was Anna and Josephine

at that point
Mr. Berkovitz abruptly turns around
and leaves the room
Mrs. Berkovitz motions me outside
and whispers
my husband is still looking for lost relatives
ever since he first saw you
he had detected a family resemblance
and even though I told him
it was impossible
he persisted
I am sorry
she says
that he bothered you
but the names aren't right

Mrs. Berkovitz quietly closes the door
and I
I run from the building
the German gentile
followed by the sorrow and despair
of Mr. and Mrs. Berkovitz
still looking

As You Wish Madam

in 1944
mother and daughter
aged forty-nine and nineteen
live in a tiny kitchen
in the overcrowded ghetto
into which the Nazis
have crammed all Jews
from the entire district

each morning
they fold their bedding
so that the other nine people
who live in the tiny adjoining room
can cook their meals
with whatever meager rations
are still allotted to them

rumors are rampant
about what was going
to happen to them
in the future
and every day
is lived in fear

the daughter had declined
an offer to be hidden
by a farmer
who told her
that nobody would suspect her
of being Jewish

because of her blond hair
and blue eyes

but how could she abandon her mother
who was widowed
and had no other relatives
nearby

one early morning
they hear the dreaded sound
of heavy boots running up the stairs
the local police
under orders from the SS
knock on doors
give everybody five minutes
to pack one suitcase
and to go to the marketplace
from where they are ordered
by the SS
to walk to the railroad station
and the entire Jewish population of
the town of Munkacs in Hungary
and surrounding area
is shoved into cattle cars

for three days and nights
they ride in the train
without food or water
until they arrive in Auschwitz

an SS man with a bullhorn
gives instructions in German

tell me
the mother asks her daughter
tell me
what the man with the bullhorn is saying

the daughter
who had learned German at school
listens to the man with the bullhorn
amidst crying children
and the confusion
of thousands of terrified Jews
pouring out of cattle cars

he is saying
the daughter says to her mother
whose raven black hair
has turned white in large patches
during the three days and nights
in the cattle car
he is saying
that we have to run ten kilometers
and that all those who are over fifty
or sick
can take a bus

the mother looks at her inadequate footwear
and the heavy suitcase
and tells her daughter
she can't run ten kilometers
shouldn't she ask permission
to use the bus
even though she is only forty-nine

the idea of separating
terrifies them both
but the daughter feels sorry
for her worn-out mother
and persuades her it would be best
to take the bus

fearfully
the daughter approaches
one of the black-booted SS men
the one in charge
later identified as Dr. Mengele
tells him
that her mother is not sick
and only forty-nine
but very tired
and could she please use the bus

as you wish Madam
the SS man says
courteously
with a slight bow

much relieved
the mother boards the bus

see you in a few hours
the daughter says
and gets ready
for the ten-kilometer run

but they don't have to run
after all

and the daughter learns
that the German word *laufen*
means both running and walking
when she arrives in Auschwitz-Birkenau
a few hours later

there's no sign of the bus
and her mother

repeated enquiries result in shrugs
but the next day
one of the guards
points to the thick smoke
coming out of the chimney
and tells the nineteen-year-old
there — that's your mother

If Only I Had Known

her mother was
one of the survivors
liberated in January 1945
from Auschwitz
she herself was born in a
displaced persons camp in Germany
in 1947
and whenever the talk turned to her grandmother
there was a hesitancy a vagueness
how grandma had died

forty-nine years later
after seeing *Schindler's List*
the mother calls her daughter
now living in a picturesque town
on the shoreline in New England
and tells her
choking on tears
that she caused her mother's death
because she hadn't known
that the German word *laufen*
meant both running and walking
and she had advised her mother
to take the bus
reserved for those
who were ill
and over fifty
even though her mother was only forty-nine
and not ill
only dreadfully tired

and terrified
of a ten-kilometer run
in inadequate shoes
with the heavy suitcase

the bus delivered her mother
straight into the gas chambers
with all the others who were sick
and over fifty years old

before the SS emptied the ghetto
she had rejected an offer
by Christian neighbors
to be hidden on a farm
in the country
it'll be so easy
they told her
nobody will suspect
that you are Jewish
with your blond hair
and blue eyes

but she told them
that she couldn't desert
her widowed mother
her mother needed her

and then I sent her to her death
within days of our deportation
she says
stunned by her own words
spoken for the first time
aloud

in almost fifty years
if only I had known German better
she continues
if only I had known their system

Mom
the daughter interrupts
Mom
the Nazis killed Grandma
not you
not your lack of knowledge of the German language
not your overall nineteen-year-old ignorance

if only I had known
the mother continues
over and over
sobbing uncontrollably
if only I had known

How I Learned to Cook

what did you talk about
all day
I ask my friend Judith
fifty years after her liberation from Auschwitz
who told me
that the daily ration of food
was a few spoonfuls of revolting soup
and one piece of bread

did you talk about your fears of dying
the fate of your family or relatives
how all this had come about
the insanity of it all

oh no
she says
none of that
we talked about food mostly
and recipes

how to make the best Hungarian goulash
delectable stuffed cabbage
the most flavorful chicken soup
the smoothest gravies
and the best cakes

that's how I learned
how to make high-rising yeast dough
pound cake that wouldn't collapse
tortes filled and decorated with butter cream

when my mother wanted
to teach me cooking
at home
I'd tell her that I didn't need to learn that
I'd have a maid
when i was grown up

in Auschwitz
I learned how important it is
to gently fold the flour into the beaten eggs
for a successful pound cake
and how you can't rush a yeast dough
it needs time to rise

the women
talked about
how you could make three different cakes
with the same dough
by cutting it into three portions —
rolling out one portion
covering it with a mixture of cocoa and sugar
then rolling it up lengthwise
and placing on a baking sheet

you'd roll out the second portion of dough
cover with a mixture of sugared poppy seed
and treat like number one

finally
you'd roll out the third portion
cut into halves
cover one half with a mixture
of farmer's cheese eggs raisins and sugar

place the second half on top
tuck in the sides
let all three cakes rise again
and bake

there were lengthy debates
about the preference of Czech dumplings
made from a light yeast dough
over Hungarian dumplings
made from flour and eggs
with a crouton inside
to serve with the goulash

the women emphasized
that an old chicken
makes a more flavorful soup
than a young one
but that the adding of plenty of root vegetables
plus onions and celery
is equally important

that's how I learned to cook
she repeats
both of us salivating
at the memory of those imagined dishes
in Auschwitz-Birkenau
fifty-one years ago

Her Friend Sophie
RECOLLECTIONS OF AN AUSCHWITZ SURVIVOR

in January 1945
   ten days
after the German guards
forced all who could walk
to leave Auschwitz with them
(many of those to be shot dead on the way)
leaving the sick behind
to fend for ourselves
without food water and electricity
but full of hope
because we knew the end of terror was near
   seven days
after the Gestapo
showed up for a day
unexpectedly
ordered everybody to leave the barracks
at once
or else be burned alive
with the barracks
while I warned
as many as I could reach
to hold out
and not to follow those orders
but to stay hidden inside the barracks
where we huddled for the rest of the day and night
until the Gestapo left
and we found all those
who had followed the orders

shot to death
near the gates
   three days
after the German army
fleeing from the victorious Russians
tried to persuade us
to come with them
to save us from the Russians
and we told them
are you crazy
we are eagerly waiting for the Russians
to liberate us
   one day
after the Russians arrived
and fed us kasha
as much as we wanted
all of us
were sick with severe diarrhea
from the unaccustomed richness
and quantity of food

I found my friend Sophie
in a coma
reeking with vomit and excrement

nobody wanted to touch her
typhoid was rampant
but my friends helped me
to get scissors rags clean clothes
and warm water

I cut the soiled clothes
peeled them off Sophie's body

and washed her
gently
from head to toe
I dried her
dressed her in clean clothes
put her down
in a bunk with a clean straw mattress

at that moment
Sophie opened her eyes
and said
how nice I can see again

Sophie was such a pretty girl
even though she was all skin and bones
she had the most beautiful eyes
and I told her
not to eat any more kasha
and that I'd be back
with a bit of toast

when I came back
half an hour later
with the precious toast
Sophie sat in the same position
I left her
propped up against the straw mattress
those beautiful eyes closed
dead

half of us died within days
after being liberated

we were so sick
so unaccustomed to rich food

I wished
I could have saved Sophie
she says
then sits up straight
and says firmly
at least she died clean
I am happy for that

The Price of Gold

one year after her liberation from Auschwitz
after an entire year spent in a hospital in Sweden
still dangerously thin
the doctor tells her
about a benefactor and his family
who have invited her for Passover
a month from now
provided
the doctor adds
that she will gain enough weight by then

the sixteen-year-old
who spent two years in Auschwitz
and has been confined to the hospital
since her release
desperately wants to spend Passover
with the family of the benefactor

she tries to eat as much as possible
but her intestines are still compromised
from the two years of severe starvation
and nothing seems to stick to her

every day
the nurse weighs her
but she doesn't achieve the required weight
until one day before Passover
and the doctor says
you may go

hurriedly
someone sews her a dress
ill fitting
because of the haste
but a new dress nevertheless
and she goes to the house
of the benefactor and his family

they live in an elegant apartment building
with an elevator
but the elevator scares her
instead she walks up five flights
stands in front of the door
looks at the doorbell
realizes she is empty handed
turns abruptly
descends the stairs
leaves the building
walks the streets
to find a flower shop
and buys a bouquet of flowers
for the benefactor
and his family

back she goes
again shies away from the elevator
despite feeling faint
but cannot overcome her panic
of being confined in a small space
in unknown territory
reaches the fifth floor
rings the doorbell

a maid opens the door
takes the flowers
and shows her into a room
so she can change

she stands in the room
looks around
and doesn't know what to do —
the ill-fitting dress
is all she has

finally
she meets the benefactor
and his family
and is invited to sit down at the table
beautifully set
to celebrate her first Seder
since her deportation
to Auschwitz

soon
the talk turns to gold
the price of gold on the world market
to be exact
and the sixteen-year-old
who was liberated from Auschwitz
twelve months ago
near death
whose parents and most of her family were murdered
who has been confined to a hospital ever since
who has looked forward to this day
for months
who has dreamed of being in the outside world

with normal people
for so long
and participating in this familiar religious ceremony
among her people
is shocked that
the topic of conversation
quickly turned to matters so mundane

there is nothing
she can contribute
to a conversation
about the price of gold

she gets up
goes to the door
opens it
steps outside
quietly closes the door behind her
avoids the elevator
walks down the five flights of stairs
leaves the building
and walks the streets of Stockholm
a foreign city to her
on this first day of real freedom
in three years
on Passover 1946

Still Haunted

he had a budding law practice
lots of friends
a lovely lady friend
and thoroughly enjoyed
life in the cosmopolitan city of Berlin

still
he had read *Mein Kampf*
and when Hitler came to power
in nineteen thirty-three
he gave up his law practice
without any hesitation
and returned to his native Vienna

shortly thereafter
he woke up one morning
from a terrible nightmare —
he had seen a cattle truck
drive by his house
in a residential area
filled with Jews
desperate
screaming
begging passersby
to help them

all day
Eric thought about
what he was supposed to do

after all
it was only a dream

but the haunting images
and the sense of impending doom
followed him for days
and since he knew
what Hitler had spelled out
so clearly in his writing
he finally went to the office of B'nai B'rith
and told the director
that something horrible
was going to happen to the Jews in Europe
and that it was important
to do everything possible
to prevent this catastrophe

the director assured him
that he and directors of similar agencies
were well informed about Hitler's intentions
and were prepared for all contingencies

much relieved
Eric went home

five and a half years later
after the Annexation of Austria
to Hitler's Germany
he fled his native country
in fear of being sent to
a concentration camp
and narrowly escaped death

sixty-one years later
ninety-two year old Eric
is still haunted by his dream

he continuously asks himself
why he had this dream
and wonders
how many lives
could have been saved
had he insisted
on more drastic action
by the appropriate Jewish agencies
and what he could have done
should have done
to prevent the slaughter
of so many

In the Shower

shortly after Hitler's Annexation of Austria
after the confiscation of businesses and homes
owned by Jews
after witnessing an orthodox Jew
in payess scull cap and caftan
being used as a punching ball
by a group of laughing SS on the street
while Austrian gentiles stood by
and months of increasing fear
of being arrested
and taken to a concentration camp
Walter managed to get an affidavit
from a distant relative in the USA
and he and his wife
sailed to New York in 1938

immediately
they began looking
for sponsors who could give them affidavits
for his three sisters
who had been able to escape to France
where they were illegal refugees
and for their parents
who were still in Vienna
unable to leave
unless they had visas
for a country
willing to take them

sponsors had to prove
they could support
those they sponsored
but money
was hard to make
for refugees
who had trouble speaking the language
and whose professions were often useless

still
eventually
the three sisters
were safely in the States
and all worked hard
to save money
for their parents' visas and boat fare

month after month went by
filling out application forms
learning about quotas
running from agency to agency
and always being told
that there wasn't enough money
and consequently no visas

one day
Walter came home
and saw his wife
had bought some decoration
for the kitchen
it only cost a quarter
she said

apologetically
even a quarter is too much
he yelled
we cannot spend
will not spend
a penny on nonessentials
until our parents are safe

after three years
of saving and scrimping
after battling with immigration regulations
of half a dozen countries
Walter and his wife
were able to get a loan
from an American friend
and were overjoyed to finally secure
visas to Cuba
for their parents
for a substantial amount of money
through the friend of a brother-in-law
whose cousin was living there

just then
the States declared war on Germany
and the visas became useless

they never heard from their parents again
after 1942
and only learned
after the war
that they had been killed
in a concentration camp

every morning
when he takes a shower
eighty-nine-year-old Walter
thinks of his parents
and the horrible deaths
they suffered
fifty-two years ago

The Golden Childhood

in their teens
they all envied Debbie
and her doting
indulgent mother

Debbie was an only child
didn't have to share toys with siblings
was allowed to request her favorite dishes
every day
could change her mind
after her mother brought the favorite dish to the table
and request another one
which her mother dutifully cooked
immediately
and that one didn't have to be eaten either
if Debbie changed her mind
again

Debbie was the height of fashion
in her pretty clothes
sported a new expensive bike
when the rest of them made do
with second-hand acquisitions

Debbie had her own room
with lovely girlish furniture
while most of them struggled
with sofabeds in the living room
and could only dream of a room of their own

Debbie always had money for movies
in fact was allowed to see any movie she wanted
didn't seem to suffer under unreasonable curfews
and was allowed to stay over
at friends' houses
as often as she pleased
while they were not allowed
out of their parents' sight

besides
Debbie's mother was always dressed impeccably
and cut an elegant
cosmopolitan figure

most of their parents
were not well dressed
were often sickly
suffocated them with overprotective love
had spent years in displaced persons camps
eked out modest livelihoods
with tentative tiny businesses
or lived on welfare
while waiting for compensation money
from the German government
in Frankfurt Germany
fifteen years after the end of WWII
and the gruesome discovery of what had happened
to the Jews
in concentration camps

they all knew
that Debbie had
a perfect childhood

she was the secret object
of their fantasies

thirty years later
they meet again
at a friend's house
during a rare visit to Germany

Debbie looks old for her age
has recently been diagnosed
with a chronic intestinal illness
has trouble walking
chain-smokes
never married
has no children

the conversation is tentative
careful
how to measure up
in the attainments of dreams

two bottles of wine later
in the small hours of the morning
defenses down
from fatigue
and the desire
to find commonality in their lives
now lived in different countries
the talk turns to their parents
all dead now

some of them had had elderly parents
they had been the second family

after the first one had been murdered
in concentration camps
others' parents had been unwell for the rest of their lives
after the hardships they had suffered
one father had committed suicide
after a nervous breakdown
and several commitments to a mental institution
Debbie's mother had died at sixty of heart disease
her father had followed suit within the year
at fifty-nine
and made Debbie an orphan at twenty-six

there were few other relatives

suddenly
one of them remembers
Debbie's golden childhood —
the subject of their past envy

Debbie looks at them all
and says
do you know what it was like
to hear Auschwitz stories
on my mother's lap
day after day
when other children heard fairy tales
of big bad wolves
and little girls being saved
by noble creatures

RIGHT didn't simply mean an identification
of the hand used for writing

as opposed to the LEFT hand
which was used to hold the fork in proper table manners
RIGHT meant death
LEFT meant a temporary reprieve
the word SELECTION was a word
my mother used over and over again
and of course RAMP
as in being on the RAMP during SELECTION
the words GAS CHAMBERS
invariably led to the story
how one day
she too
was ordered to the RIGHT
and was sent to the gas chamber
but then they were all led out again
later on
something had gone wrong
no gassing that day —
wasn't it a miracle
she would ask her tiny daughter
that she wasn't killed

her mother
a slight woman
told little Debbie
that every day
they were taken to the woods
to cut down trees
they froze in winter
in thin clothes
and suffered many fatal accidents
none of them was skilled
in this type of work

to this day
Debbie is scared of woods
and much prefers the safety of cities
the asphalt sidewalks
the comfort of towering buildings
the mass of concrete steel and glass
to the fragrance of moss and leaves
which reminds her of the smell of death
and to swaying trees
which could topple and crush her

no stories
please
I would beg my mother
silently
Debbie says
and then I'd try to close my ears
pretend not to hear anything
when the key word Auschwitz
was mentioned
again and again

I was my mother's lifeline
Debbie explains
I was her confidante
her best friend
her reason for being alive
her connection to the outside world
her mother
to whom she recounted her life's trauma
over and over

always asking me
her child
the substitute for her dead mother
how was it that she lived
and everybody else was killed

They Kept Asking

when my grown-up daughters
meet my friend Dalia
who lives in Jerusalem
they tell her
how much they enjoyed
their recent visit to Israel
and how wonderful it was
to get to know
and spend time
with their cousins
aunt and uncle there

were you born in Israel
they ask my friend Dalia
no no she says
I was born in Vienna
more questions follow
as to how and why
she came to live in Israel
finally
after much prodding
she tells them
how she left Vienna
at thirteen
alone
on the last boat
allowed to enter Palestine
in 1939

what about your parents
they want to know
did they follow later
no Dalia says
I never saw them again
what about other relatives
they ask
nobody survived
Dalia says quietly
and adds
when she sees
tears in my daughters eyes
I didn't suffer so much

Dalia turns to me
and says
apologetically
I didn't want to tell them
but they kept asking
really she says
more and more distraught now
I didn't mean to upset them

Dalia
I say firmly
swallowing my own tears
it's not your fault
that your family was killed
and there is nothing wrong
with my daughters
crying
over what happened to you
at age thirteen

oblivious to my words
Dalia stands in the middle of the room
looks from me
to my crying daughters
and keeps saying
I didn't want to tell them
but they kept asking

The SS on the Trains

fifty-four years
after she left Austria
her native land
at age thirteen
alone
on the last boat
to enter Palestine
to escape
mass executions by Nazis
and never saw any
of her family again
she shows her husband
who suffered a similar fate
but never talks about the past
several sketches
for a piece of jewelry
she plans to execute —
definitely not the top right
he says firmly

surprised at her husband
normally so supportive
of all her artistic endeavors
she asks
and why not that one

don't you remember
he says
pointing to two zigzag lines
in the sketch on the top right
the SS on the trains

Guests of Honor

when Mr. and Mrs. Schupler
first received the official letter
from Germany
there was a moment
of panic

there had been other official German letters
sixty years ago —
letters which deprived them
of their citizenship
even though Mrs. Schupler's father
had fought in WWI
had won a medal
and Mr. Schupler's father had been
a well-known scientist
and both families
had lived in Germany
for over five hundred years

those letters had informed them
in cold and exact language
that they were not allowed
to hold jobs
own their home
live in apartment buildings
where Aryans lived
and had to add Sara and Israel
to their given names
so that they would be easily identifiable
immediately

by anyone
as Jews

in the end
they had been the lucky ones —
a distant cousin
in the United States
had sponsored them
and even though
they were not allowed
to take any money with them
and the first few years
had been spent in grinding poverty
living in run-down rooming houses
with futile searches for jobs —
Heinrich's training as a lawyer
had been useless
and Charlotte
a trained musician
raised with a maid
cook and gardener
had been equally unsuccessful
there were plenty of maids and nannies
who were more qualified than she

eventually
their distant cousin
had helped them
set up a business
with novelty items
and after years
of long working hours
and dogged persistence

they had become
moderately successful
and had managed
to send their two American-born sons
to a good university

there had been letters
from Germany
after the war
which told them
in response to their inquiries
that their parents
had been *lost* in Auschwitz
they were given an exact date
of their *disappearance* in Auschwitz
but the official letter
did not give
the cause of death

it made them so angry
nobody got lost in Auschwitz
they exclaimed
people were murdered in Auschwitz
by being beaten to death
gassed
starved
or they died as victims
of unimaginable medical experiments

then there were the years of letters
exchanged with the German government
in response to their requests
for compensation

for their home
the demolished careers

how to put a dollar amount
on the years of anguish
the humiliation
and the murder
of their parents
most of their aunts uncles cousins
and friends

there was always
a request
for yet another document —
how to prove
that they had been forced
to sell the family home
for next to nothing
how much Heinrich's law practice
had been worth
all files had been burned
when his office was ransacked
and how to prove
that Mrs. Schupler
would have been
a successful violinist

eventually
they were awarded a small pension
and received some money
for their home —
they were both relieved
to be finished

with the tiresome
correspondence

there had been no further letters
from Germany
for many years

this letter
from the Mayor of Danneburg
invited them both
in formal and exact language
to be the guests of honor
at a celebration
to welcome home
all former residents
who had been chased out of Germany
by the Nazi regime

Mr. and Mrs. Schupler
were stunned at first
then thought about
what to do —
to accept or not to accept
to go back to the place
of their pain
their losses
their humiliation
even though the letter
clearly stated
they would be guests of honor
of the whole town
the plane ticket
and rooms at the best hotel

paid for
all meals on the house
and how happy the town would be
to show *Herr und Frau* Schupler
what happened
more than fifty years ago
had been a terrible aberration
and how eager the citizens were
to show the former residents
they were
a humane and caring country

to Mr. and Mrs. Schupler
the real temptation
of the invitation to Germany
was not the offer
of being guests of honor
but the opportunity
to see old friends
classmates
neighbors' children
with whom they had played
a long time ago

finally
after going back and forth
and changing their minds
a hundred times
they had accepted the invitation
and were guests of honor
at a week-long series
of official events —
the opening of a museum

the dedication of a new high school
to those who had resisted the Nazi regime
a park named after a Jewish citizen
and Mr. and Mrs. Schupler were given
keys to the town
by the Mayor
at the most elaborate ceremony
of them all
with the television and press in attendance

they sat through fine speeches
a little dazed
by all the attention
given to them
but eventually had the opportunity
to contact old classmates
friends from law school
and the conservatory

none of them asked Mr. and Mrs. Schupler
how they had managed in their new country
after escaping Germany
whether Heinrich had been able
to build up a new law practice
whether Charlotte had been able
to pursue her musical career
none of them asked
what had become of their parents
aunts uncles and cousins
none of them asked
how it felt
to be back in Germany
after so many years

and the horrible things done to them
and their families

instead
they talked about the hardships
they had suffered —
how the Allied Forces
had bombed their city
to smithereens
how hungry they had been
at the end of the war
and for several years after the war
how many of their men
didn't come back
from the eastern front
how many of those coming back
had missing limbs
how many civilians died of typhoid
how hard they had worked to remove
the rubble
and to rebuild their city
and how nobody wanted to acknowledge
that they too had been victims
of the Hitler regime

The Old Woman

she's an old woman now
my former teacher
the noted goldsmith and ivory carver
who left her native land
war-torn Germany
in the fifties
to have a better life
for herself and her two sons
in the United States of America

the old woman is lonely
in her beautiful house in Duck Hill
surrounded by rare flowers
a pond with water lilies
a patch of raspberry bushes
columbines in white pink and purple
and eagerly tells me about her life

my father had a small print shop in Breslau
she says
and was a socialist
my mother had been a pretty maid
and remained a staunch supporter of the monarchy
all her life
they used to beat each other
then beat us children
my brother and me

he was three years older than I
and became a history professor

I enrolled at the Breslau Art Academy
and fell in love with the ancient art
of turning precious metals
and stones into jewelry
at twenty-five
I had saved enough money
to travel to the Far East
and bought hand-embroidered silk underwear
then I lived in Spain for a year
among refugees from Hitler's Germany

but my mother was dying
and I returned to Breslau
to say good-bye to her
after she died
I married my teacher the professor —
he had courted me
with bouquets of exotic flowers
and tickets to the opera
he was twelve years my senior
and this was his third marriage

he changed as soon as we were married
ordered me around
beat me
insisted on separate bedrooms
we never really slept together
he used to come visit me
but would always return to his own room afterwards

what did you expect of marriage
I ask her

I don't think I had any expectations
she says
nothing that I remember
the courtship had dazzled me so
with bouquets of exotic flowers
and tickets to the opera
he was known as the distinguished professor
I was the daughter
of a small print shop owner
and a pretty maid

after my first son was born
my husband started an affair with my best friend
shortly thereafter
my brother committed suicide
he had been in love with a Jewish girl
and saw no hope for the future

my brother was so overbred
she says
using a Nazi term
that most people reserve
for describing horses and such

then the war started
she continues
I had another son
he was my favorite
so full of life and spunk
when the Russians came
my husband took off with his mistress
and left us to fend for ourselves

they raped me
but eventually we were able
to flee to the West

when I came to America
a man courted me
and went down on his knees
to propose to me
imagine
she says
he went down on his knees
in vain I wait
to hear more about the man who loved her
was he handsome
kind
honest
affectionate
when I flew back to Germany
she continues
to settle my affairs before the planned wedding
my fiancé died of a heart attack

five years later
my favorite son
married at nineteen
against my will
had a baby
needed extra money for his young family and his studies
and drove sports cars to the West Coast
but one day his car was hit by a truck
and he died
my other son
the one who had always been dependable

returned to Austria
with his young wife
to raise a family there

the old woman in Duck Hill has become stingy
even though she has accumulated
a tidy amount of money with clever real estate dealings
and some good investments
she counts the potatoes she eats
denies herself fresh fruit and vegetables
and when I come to visit
and bring lunch enough for two
and leftovers for her dinner
I can read in her eyes
another dollar and twenty-seven cents saved today

she tells me
that her grandson
the favorite dead son's son
whom she hardly knew
(she had hated her daughter-in-law)
had shown up unexpectedly at her doorstep —
at first she enjoyed the young life in her empty house
but the tall young man
who had been a bouncer in a bar in Louisiana
and was full of outrageous stories and pipe dreams
used too much hot water for his daily shower
and had a healthy appetite
can you imagine
she says
how much the electricity cost
for all that hot water he used
and the three big meals a day

she told him
he had to leave
and the grandson joined the army

the old woman in Duck Hill
who had talked to me at length
about the horror of war
says
they'll make a real man out of him there
and they'll teach him discipline

the noted goldsmith and ivory carver
has a fine library of art books
and when we pore over books
full of dazzling treasures
from the times of Alexander the Great
she says
all this was created with the help of slaves —
pity we don't have slaves anymore

the old woman in Duck Hill
the noted goldsmith and ivory carver
who was beaten by her parents
whose only brother committed suicide
whose husband hit her
and betrayed her with her best friend
whose favorite son died in a car accident
because she wouldn't give him the money
he needed for his young family
whose devoted fiancé died of a heart attack
the old woman in Duck Hill
is very lonely

The Socialist

as a young man
in the twenties
in Germany
he joined the youth movement
with enthusiasm

back to nature
was the word of the day
for himself and his comrades
they shed starched collars
restrictive clothing
wore comfortable shoes in winter
sandals in summer
hiked through the mountains
built canoes and explored rivers and lakes
slept in homemade tents
ate wholesome food
cooked on campfires
and sang
old folk songs
at sunset

unnatural
was the word
most often used
to describe their parents' way of life
decadent
the world
they openly defied

in due course
the young man
added socialism
to his passions —
better wages
health insurance
maternity leave
a shorter work week
annual vacation
labor unions
and the right to strike
were issues
he and his comrades
discussed endlessly
they were going to create
a better world
with fairness
equality
and justice

most of them were pacifists
but antisemitism
and racism
were not part of their concerns

when he married the girl
with whom he had hiked
through the mountains
with whom he had explored rivers
and lakes in a canoe
and with whom he had sung folk songs
while watching sunsets
he became her master —

he told her what clothes to wear
how to do her hair
and doled out a meager allowance
for household expenses
each week
for which she had to account
seven cents for milk on Monday
sixty-seven cents spent for flour
sugar and margarine on Tuesday
it never tallied up right on Saturday
when he requested to see her account book
somehow she always forgot to write down
an item or two

she desperately tried to remember
what the missing quarter had been spent on
detergent
potatoes
cabbage
while he interrogated her
relentlessly
come on now
you must remember
his voice getting louder
and louder
and she
terrified
started to cry
remembering all the while
what the nuns and the priest had told her
in the convent where girls from good families
had been educated
you must always obey your husband

then the children arrived
one every eleven months
till there were seven
and the socialist father
who continued going to union meetings
became a tyrant to them all
now he had a wife
and three daughters
whose hairdos and clothing he could dictate
and four sons
whom he could order around

he firmly believed
that children were born bad
to the core
and had to be beaten
often
and thoroughly
to turn them
into functioning human beings

the socialist father
vehemently opposed to Hitler
and the Thousand Year Reich
nevertheless believed
in Hitler's gene theory
he was always accusing his children
of taking after (bad) Uncle Harry
and (bad) Aunt Edith
the socialist father
had no compassion
for physical afflictions
or weaknesses

and called his asthmatic son
a damned cripple

the socialist father
who dreamed of a better world
where justice would reign
equality
and fairness
instituted a system of special favors
for reporting infractions committed
by other siblings
and created an atmosphere
of distrust
fear
and betrayal

the father
who firmly and passionately believed
that socialism would save the world
never considered
his children's needs
for affection
kindness
counsel
good role models
and their right to choose
what clothes to wear
what courses to take at school
and what careers to pursue

at seventy-five
the socialist
died a bitter old man

he wasn't bitter
because his dreams
of a better world hadn't come true
or because he and his comrades
hadn't been able to prevent WWII
or the Holocaust
the old socialist was bitter
because all of his four sons
two of whom were physicians
one a professor
one a science librarian
had not obeyed his orders
to become engineers like himself
and because his daughters
one a surgeon
one a businesswoman
one an artist
had defied his orders
to choose careers
he considered
suitable for women

My Cousin Theo

for years I heard
that Cousin Theo
wasn't put together quite right

talk about Cousin Theo
was never specific
or direct
and was done in whispers
with plenty of insinuations
and things unsaid
Theo after all
was the son
of a brilliant and respected physician
and had three normal brothers and sisters

Cousin Theo was hidden
by his family
from the rest of us
in the attic
accessible only by back stairs

Theo is asleep
one was told
when visiting
and asking after him

rumors persisted
over the years —
Cousin Theo roamed the house at night

raided the icebox
had grown obese
turned on the radio full blast
or listened to records
hour after hour after hour —
he led an astounding existence in a country
where one's worth is based on what one does

my memory of Cousin Theo
who is five years older than I
is that of a shadow —
I couldn't remember
what he looked like
forty-five years later
on a visit
to see my family in Germany

I am surprised to hear
that Cousin Theo
is eagerly waiting to see me
I have to admit
that I never thought
about Cousin Theo
in my travels
and my efforts
to build a new life
in the United States of America
and never thought
that Cousin Theo
the shadow
ever gave
a second thought to me

Cousin Theo
the retard
who hasn't seen me in half a lifetime
recognizes me
the minute I step off the train
he runs toward me
his face breaks into a wide grin
he raises his arms
embraces me
holds me tight
then lifts me up
swirls me around and around

Cousin Theo beams and talks
he tells me minute details
from the past
about family gatherings
first communions mostly
who was present
tells me that I was a skinny little girl
with long braids
who couldn't sit still for a minute
that two of my siblings had lovely blond curls
were called cherubs by everybody
that my twin brother and I were called the darkies
and that my oldest sister
was always ordering her six siblings around

was he hovering in the background
behind half-closed doors
or on the first landing
of the staircase
when he was shunned

from those family gatherings
ready to rush upstairs
when caught
and got to know us much more
than we were allowed to know him

Cousin Theo is a short man
severely cross-eyed
wears thick owlish glasses
and is decidedly not handsome
it's true he seems
a bit of an odd fellow
but I cannot detect
any trace
of mental retardation

later I learn
from his older handsome brother
whose ward he is
that Cousin Theo
entered this world too early
and was plagued
with health problems —
he couldn't see well
and his hearing was poor
but the shame
of sending his son
to a school for handicapped children
providing him
with special education
was unacceptable
for the brilliant respected physician

Cousin Theo
stayed home
hidden from the world

I wonder
whether my uncle
took offense at his son's plainness
among his older
handsome children —
after all this was the time
of the master race

Cousin Theo received almost no education
was not taught a trade
acquired no social skills
was not allowed
to have dreams
of travel
of adventures
of life with a wife
and children of his own

later my mother
adds another twist
to Cousin Theo's story —
Theo's mother had had a brother
who was emotionally unstable
he couldn't control his temper
had threatened a neighbor with a knife once
it was said —
unacceptable behavior
in a country

based on
obedience and conformity
so he was committed
to a mental institution

one day
Theo's mother
received an official document
and an urn
the document stated
that her brother
(who was in the prime of his life
and in excellent health)
had suddenly died of pneumonia
and the urn contained his ashes

Cousin Theo's parents
have both passed away
will he ever know
whether he was hidden
because of his father's shame
or to save his life
from Hitler's use of euthanasia
against those who didn't fit
the image of the master race

Das Thema

(THE TOPIC)

I have had it up to here
with *DAS THEMA*
the young woman
in Germany
tells me
angrily
while motioning to
an imaginary line
above her head

when I plead ignorance
and ask
the young woman
what topic she's referring to
she looks at me in disbelief —
surely I must know
what she means
everybody does

no I don't
I answer
you forget
that I live in the States
and not in Germany
and am not up
on the current use
of encrypted language

the young woman
is stunned
but then spurts out
the Nazi regime
of course
and the Holocaust

why don't *they* stop
talking about IT
she adds
vehemently
who are *they*
I want to know

more fluster ensues

the young woman
whose children's great-grandfather
was hanged
in Dachau
because he opposed
the Hitler regime
looks at me
with narrowed eyes
and says
the Jews of course

where do they talk
about IT
I inquire further

don't you know
she says

getting more and more
agitated
on television
on the radio
and in the newspapers

that's all you hear
see and read
she states
you can't open the newspapers
turn on the radio
open a magazine or newspaper
without reading or hearing
about IT

so the Jews
control German television
the radio stations
and the press
I ask
and then express
my surprise
that such a tiny minority
has achieved
such exceptional power

there were only
thirty thousand of them
until just a few years ago
I tell the young woman
true
another twenty thousand Jews from Russia
have since made their home in Germany

but I assume
I continue
that the Russian Jews
hardly know enough German
to control the media in Germany

but the young woman
does not think
it's unlikely
that a tiny minority
of less than
zero point zero three seven five percent
has that much power

a few weeks later
the director of a prestigious
German institution in Israel
tells me
that people in the United States
may be interested in *DAS THEMA*
but not people in Israel

Weather Report

another month or two
at the most
my brother had told me
in July
the cancer had come back
with a vengeance
and was growing aggressively

she was done with fancy medical treatment
she said
eighty-four is a good age
twice in intensive care
within eighteen months
after major surgery
for weeks on end
hooked up to machines
tubes sticking out every which way
it's enough
she said
I want to go home

there was no safe topic
between my mother and me
which we could tackle
without fear
so over the following months
of twice-weekly phone calls
from the safe distance
of three thousand miles
across the ocean

we discussed
the weather

first it was general statements —
it's sunny today
or
the sky is overcast over here
but slowly
we were caught by
the transcontinental weather dramas —
it's the most miserably cold summer in decades
she would say
while I kept her informed
about the seventh week of our summer drought
and described
how everything was wilting
even the weeds
besides the water in the well was getting low
not enough water for watering
my vegetable and flower gardens

in Cologne
in the meantime
the weeks of rain
were unexpectedly interrupted
by some warm and sunny days —
what a nice surprise
she reported
while across the Atlantic
we were finally drowning in heavy rain
which in turn
led to a report of a leak in the roof

passion entered our vocabulary
when we described the extremes
in the weather patterns
that plagued two different continents
in that fall
when she was dying

at times
I found myself scanning the weather channel
so I could add weather predictions
to my reports —
it's pleasant today
I would say
but there's a front moving
across the country
expected to be here by midweek
and a nasty storm brewing in the Pacific —
which should get here this weekend

eventually
my mother and I
who had never had a real conversation
with each other
always disagreed about everything
had fought endlessly
had rubbed each other raw with words
achieved an odd sense of intimacy
in those talks about the weather
we felt close
we felt trust
we felt peace

the weather
in all its unpredictability
its fickleness
had provided a safe haven

and then she died
in early November

since then
we've had a colder than usual December
enormous snowfall in January and February
and are breaking hundred-year records
in temperature lows —
so much to report
but I can't call her anymore

Footbinding

when I grew up in Germany
in the forties and fifties
my mother told me plenty of stories
about the restrictions and cruelties
women in faraway countries had to endure —
in some countries
women had to cover themselves
from head to toe in black garments
in others
women were kept locked up in houses
surrounded by high walls
my mother knew of one tribe
which forced its girls to marry several husbands
and on Friday
at high noon
women who were said to have committed adultery
were hanged
in the open marketplace
in one particularly dark part of the world

we lived in a civilized country
advanced
fair
just

isn't it wonderful
my mother used to say
that we live
in the enlightened West
and not in some backward country

footbinding in China
was often used as an example of particular barbarity
by my mother
and
she would add
how can mothers do something
so cruel to their own daughters

yet
not a day would go by
that my mother wouldn't explain
to me
again and again
patiently
that in a good marriage
one partner has to be the hammer
while the other should be the anvil
explaining further
that men were destined
to be hammers
and women uniquely fashioned
to be anvils

the sooner you get used to it
the better
she'd say
there's no use in fighting nature

footbinding

Daddy doesn't want you to learn Latin
my mother told me at twelve
because

Latin is a language which requires logic
only men can think logically
we women shouldn't try to act like them

I know you girls have trouble understanding
math physics and chemistry
the male science teacher at the all-girls' school
told us
at the beginning of each science class
year after year
while our eyes glazed over
and our heads filled with female stupidity
still
he added cheerfully
it's part of the required curriculum
and we have to do the best we can

footbinding

women are incapable of learning how to drive
my father categorically declared
frequently
and if they do it anyway
they make lousy drivers
and are a hazard on the street

child
my mother said
in that peculiar tone
she used
when she caught me
trying to do boys' stuff
child

she said
why are you trying to read
the front page of the newspaper
with stories about politics
don't you know that women
can't understand those things
how many more times
do I have to tell you
that you need logic
something women don't have
to understand politics

footbinding

then came the time
when my long quick strides needed curtailment
and had to be retrained
into a hesitant more ladylike step —
I was handed narrow skirts
along with strict orders
not to rip the seams

what do you mean
my mother asked
incredulous
when I told her that I wanted to travel
to the south of France
with the Girl Scouts
considering that my brothers were hitchhiking
freely
all over Europe
alone

don't you understand
that that's impossible for girls to do

true
my mother didn't bind my feet
I was not required to don a chador
when I left the house
nor was our house surrounded by a high wall
and no public hangings
took place
in the marketplace
on Friday
at high noon
still
the high pitched sound of the hammer
hitting the anvil
has followed me halfway around the world

Who Knew the Murderers

where are you from
the Auschwitz survivor
who has given a lecture
on the importance
of hearing stories of survivors
asks me
after I tell her
how moved I was
by her words

Germany
I tell her
Germany
she asks
how did you survive
I am not Jewish
I answer

the Auschwitz survivor
looks me straight in the eyes
and asks
what did your father do
during the Hitler regime
my father wasn't a member of the Nazi party
and managed to avoid the draft
I answer
what about your uncles
she wants to know
they weren't Nazis either
I reply

what did they say about it
after the war
she wants to know
they didn't know about it
I tell her

it's interesting
she says
I've never met a German
whose father uncle neighbor colleague superior
was involved in the killing
or even knew about it
how was it done
she asks
looking at me intently
tell me
how do you kill six million people
with only a handful of participants
and hardly anybody knowing
you need lots of people
she says
to kill six million
lots of people
she repeats
it wasn't done
with just a handful of thugs
it took thousands of people
what am I saying
hundreds of thousands of people
to do the killing
think about it
six million
that's a lot of people to kill

even with the technology
and efficiency
the Germans mastered

ever since
I've been wondering
what my father and uncles knew
    about friends neighbors and colleagues
who of my teachers participated or knew
who printed the new laws
declaring that non-Aryans
were no longer allowed
    to live in their homes
own their own businesses
    practice medicine
    teach
    hold any kind of job
who printed the laws
forbidding Jews
    to be outside of their homes after eight in the evening
    use the telephone
    go to the theater or the movies
    eat in restaurants
    own pets
    purchase flowers
    smoke
    use a typewriter
    own fur coats
who distributed the laws and regulations
all over Germany
from the largest cities to the smallest hamlets
who translated them into different languages

who shipped them to many different countries in
Eastern Europe

who manufactured the signs
for beaches and parks
declaring
dogs and Jews not allowed

who took over
  the homes
  businesses
  medical practices
  teaching positions
  and jobs
  of the millions of non-Aryans
who wrote the long meticulous lists
  as to who was a Gypsy
  a homosexual
  a quarter Jew
  a half Jew
  a full Jew
who knew what the long lists were used for
who wrote the arrest orders
  to be carried out in the middle of the night
who worked out the complicated train schedules
  of so many trains
  going east
  day and night
  converging at the same destinations
who sewed the prison uniforms for the millions
who did research
  about the most efficient methods

of mass extermination
who collected the data from this research
　made comparisons
who made the decisions
　what methods to employ
who were the scientists
　who devised unimaginable experiments on

　　　　　　　　　　　　　　human beings

who evaluated the experiments
who wrote the reports
who signed them
who filed them
who wrote the purchase orders
　for the implements of mass murder
who manufactured the chemicals
　used for the killing
who manufactured the gas chambers
who shipped them east
who did the billing to the government

what did my parents know
who of my aunts and uncles
　teachers and neighbors knew
who knew

Not Fixable

in Germany
everything is fixable —
there is no tolerance
for anything broken
deteriorated by age
shabby
or dilapidated

a shingle missing
a nail sticking out
a loose latch on the garden door
a light bulb burned out
a tear in the curtain
a missing button
paint flaking off
rust on the car —
hammer
screwdriver
sandpaper
paintbrush
needle and thread
are always at the ready
and when something
can't be fixed anymore
it's replaced
with something new

consequently
there are few worn steps
sagging fences

weathered walls
or any signs of decay —
after all
broken things
are a sign of slovenliness
a defective character
which is considered
much worse
than being unkind

half a century
after the end of WWII
and the total devastation
of their country
there is no trace left
of the twelve years
ruled by Hitler
whom they had cheered
followed
and obeyed
whose proclamation
of their racial superiority
they had enthusiastically embraced
in whose extermination of millions
they had willingly participated
and which caused the almost
total destruction
of their own country

but to their dismay
the diligent use of
hammers

screwdrivers
paintbrushes
and sandpaper
has been ineffectual
in erasing the records
of the atrocities committed

in other countries
books are published
about the Thousand Year Reich
and memorial services held
for the victims
museums built
to confront the horrors
of the past
conventions organized
to understand
the falling of a civilized country
into barbarity

what is it you want us to do
they ask reproachfully
look at our young people
weighed down by guilt
look at the lectures organized
by the Christian-Jewish societies
the programs arranged
by the German-Israeli societies
the efforts by the third generation
undertaken with such dedication
to combat antisemitism and racism
the many sister-city connections

to towns in Israel
the many groups and individuals
who visit Israel

it makes them furious
that the outside world
(by which they mainly mean
Israel and the Jews in America)
is still focused on the past
and they are angry
that nobody wants to see
the wonderful accomplishments
of the past fifty years
in a rebuilt Germany

why is everybody still beating that dead horse
they ask angrily
and why do they refuse to forget
after all the money
we've paid them

they can't understand
that no amount of fine speeches
or good deeds
youth groups performing lowly tasks
in Israeli nursing homes
or doing backbreaking work on *kibbutzim*
town officials
issuing invitations to former citizens
to come back to their home towns
as guests of honor
lavished with attention
nothing

absolutely nothing
will erase the terrible stain
on their country's history

the stain
caused by
the one and a half million Jewish children
starved to death gassed
or shot as target practice
the four and a half million adult Jews
the hundreds of thousands of Gypsies
the Jehovah's Witnesses
the mentally and physically disabled
murdered
cannot be expunged

it's hard for them to accept —
the Holocaust
        is not forgettable
the Holocaust
        is not erasable
the Holocaust
        is not fixable

FOR THE BEST IN PAPERBACKS, LOOK FOR THE

In every corner of the world, on every subject under the sun, Penguin represents quality and variety—the very best in publishing today.

For complete information about books available from Penguin—including Puffins, Penguin Classics, and Arkana—and how to order them, write to us at the appropriate address below. Please note that for copyright reasons the selection of books varies from country to country.

In the United Kingdom: Please write to *Dept. JC, Penguin Books Ltd, FREEPOST, West Drayton, Middlesex UB7 0BR.*

If you have any difficulty in obtaining a title, please send your order with the correct money, plus ten percent for postage and packaging, to *P.O. Box No. 11, West Drayton, Middlesex UB7 0BR*

In the United States: Please write to *Consumer Sales, Penguin USA, P.O. Box 999, Dept. 17109, Bergenfield, New Jersey 07621-0120.* VISA and MasterCard holders call 1-800-253-6476 to order all Penguin titles

In Canada: Please write to *Penguin Books Canada Ltd, 10 Alcorn Avenue, Suite 300, Toronto, Ontario M4V 3B2*

In Australia: Please write to *Penguin Books Australia Ltd, P.O. Box 257, Ringwood, Victoria 3134*

In New Zealand: Please write to *Penguin Books (NZ) Ltd, Private Bag 102902, North Shore Mail Centre, Auckland 10*

In India: Please write to *Penguin Books India Pvt Ltd, 706 Eros Apartments, 56 Nehru Place, New Delhi 110 019*

In the Netherlands: Please write to *Penguin Books Netherlands bv, Postbus 3507, NL-1001 AH Amsterdam*

In Germany: Please write to *Penguin Books Deutschland GmbH, Metzlerstrasse 26, 60594 Frankfurt am Main*

In Spain: Please write to *Penguin Books S.A., Bravo Murillo 19, 1° B, 28015 Madrid*

In Italy: Please write to *Penguin Italia s.r.l., Via Felice Casati 20, I-20124 Milano*

In France: Please write to *Penguin France S.A., 17 rue Lejeune, F-31000 Toulouse*

In Japan: Please write to *Penguin Books Japan, Ishikiribashi Building, 2-5-4, Suido, Bunkyo-ku, Tokyo 112*

In Greece: Please write to *Penguin Hellas Ltd, Dimocritou 3, GR-106 71 Athens*

In South Africa: Please write to *Longman Penguin Southern Africa (Pty) Ltd, Private Bag X08, Bertsham 2013*